Day By Day
Meditations for Broken Hearts

Leslie H. Woodson

Rock of Ages Memorials

Dedication

*This book is dedicated to all who have lost,
and are mending their broken hearts.*

ISBN: 0-9722185-0-5

This book is available through Rock of Ages Memorials retailers and business partners. For details contact Rock of Ages Corporation, 369 North State Street, Concord, New Hampshire 03301 or call 1-800-884-7936.

first edition

All of us know the best way to live is day by day. That means that we do not agitate ourselves with fretting and fuming about the future until it arrives. This, of course, does not suggest that one should settle down to a life of indolence or lazy carelessness. What it does recommend is that, while the unborn years deserve some attention, there is a vast difference between planning and worrying. To be consumed with anxiety about the future is to sacrifice the claims of the present.

"What are you going to do tomorrow?" is never as urgent a question as "What are you doing today?" I am here today – tomorrow is another story.

No one knows what a day may bring, and such uncertainty makes nervous wrecks out of some of us. What this knowledge should do is encourage sensible planning for possible illness, eventual retirement and ultimate death, but it must not be permitted to render us incapable of enjoying today. To ignore possible adversity is folly, but to dwell on it is folly of an even graver sort. Plan ahead — it wasn't raining when old Noah built the ark — but do not allow yourself to get drenched before the rains begin.

This little book is designed to make it a bit easier to live one day at a time. More than likely, the rains have finally come, the floods of grief washing away much of the foundation upon which your life was built. The death of a spouse, a child, a parent or a much-loved friend is a traumatic experience of such magnitude as to leave one crushed beyond repair. Or so it seems at the time.

When the whole world comes tumbling down like a house of cards, the despair engulfs us with the fury of an emotional holocaust. The shock of one being snatched from us, without permission, wrings the tears from our eyes and the joy from our hearts. Found on the carved sarcophagus, of an Egyptian child three thousand years ago, are the words: "Oh my life, my love, my little one, would God I had died for thee." Only those who have faced such inconsolable grief can identify with the pain in that father's heart.

If it were hard to live just one day at a time before, the difficulty has now increased a hundred fold. Like the ancient Egyptian, our first thought on rising in the morning is "I've nothing more to live for," and the gnawing pain grows more intense as the night approaches. Once the word reaches us we refuse to believe it is so. It cannot be! How could one tiny second make the difference between life and death? Only a moment ago my love was with me — now he is in another world. Our minds rebel. The natural thing is to deny that what we have seen with our eyes has really happened. Nature, in her compassion, surrounds us with a numbness which insulates us from the truth. And, for this, those of us who suffer should be grateful.

Little by little you will be forced to adjust. At first, it will be slow. Time does heal. But the scars remain and they are tender for as long as you live. The empty chair at the table brings a sudden tear to you eye. The silence is deafening. The relative or friend, with whom you shared life's joys and sorrows, is no longer there to listen. But you find yourself talking anyway. And the awful loneliness . . . who can describe the fear of being all alone in a world filled with people who somehow do not count?

People reach out to you, but their loving touch does little to fill the emptiness in your aching heart. It is so easy to cry, so easy to relive the past and lose interest in the present . . . to neglect even to dress in the morning, to brood in the quietness oblivious to the world moving so quickly outside the window. Crying and wishing, sitting and dreaming – you wish you were dead. What you are experiencing is a part of the grief process common to us all. It is normal. The tragedy, however, is that too often people refuse the recovery which grief and time are designed to produce.

The following ninety pages, prepared for daily readings, will not rebuild your life overnight. They are more like time capsules which, if taken as prescribed, will slowly begin the work of restoration. Don't miss a day, and don't read ahead. Fill your mind with bright, warm thoughts ignited by the inspiration you have read. Scan the page for the day again and again – as often as you need – then, feeble as the move may be, do something which will turn your thoughts into action. Reading and thinking should motivate one to doing. Keeping your mind, your hands and your feet active is the way to begin again.

Leslie H. Woodson
Elizabethtown, Kentucky

DAY 1 ... DAY BY DAY

"Today is the first day of the rest of your life!" You have heard that so many times that it is now mundane. But it is one thing nobody can debate. This means there is something brand new about today. Even if you are a hundred years old, today is still the beginning of all that is left. You are alive at this moment and everything in the past is over and done. So, what each one of us must do is forget the past and get on with life. Fear of the future is unwarranted.

Losing a loved one can be so devastating that a person just gives up. Neither of you would have wanted the other to quit living. That would be to reject all that was good about your life together. Life does not end just because someone dies – either for him or for those left behind.

Accept this twenty-four hours as a fresh gift from God. Don't waste it. Certainly do not abuse it. And don't lose today worrying about tomorrow. The coming days can be shaped for good only if you lay the foundation for them now. Whether nineteen or ninety-one, we are all growing older. But growing older has nothing to do with the joy of living. Some of the world's most exciting people are advanced in age while others young in years have a decaying spirit.

Remember that the loved one whom you can no longer see is still walking beside you. Clasp your hands and keep walking as you always did. Together you have walked toward the sunset. Now you can walk toward the sunrise.

Whoever told you that dying puts an end to life? Well, H. G. Wells did. "Man, who began in a cave behind a windbreak," said Wells, "will end in the disease soaked ruins of a slum." How any thinking person could come to such a conclusion is difficult to ascertain.

Theodore Monod was much less negative and nearer the truth when, for his headstone, he instructed his family to chisel the words: "Here endeth the first lesson." William Cowper was seized with intermittent fits of madness, certain that he had committed an unpardonable sin. When he died, his reason in total eclipse, friends declared that there came over his face "a holy surprise."

Even Cicero, who lived nearly two millennia ago, wrote, "The nearer I approach death the more I feel like one who is in sight of land at last and is about to anchor in his home port after a long voyage . . . . I quit life as if it were an inn and not a home . . . . The soul is about to set out for a better country."

Transition is not termination. To die is to move beyond a lesser existence to a greater one. We do ourselves much harm by failing to differentiate between that which is the end and that which is only transition.

Death is never being fired . . . it is being promoted! It is being honored above your fellows left in the lower echelons of the pecking order. No one would ever reject such as advancement.

DAY 3 . . . DAY BY DAY

There is a real strength in brokenness. As a six year old boy climbing an unsupported stepladder, in an excavated area where my father was building a house, I fell and broke my left wrist. Oh, how it hurt! At the time, it seemed to me that the worst possible thing had happened and that my arm would never heal. But it did. And when the cast was removed and the use returned to my wrist, believe it or not, the strongest part of my arm was the calloused area around the old break.

Life has a way of breaking us, doesn't it? Nevertheless, it is at those points of brokenness that we are the strongest. When you have been through a severe experience which nearly tore you apart, ever afterward that is one of your strong zones. What you are now facing is possibly the hardest of all your previous struggles. But it is not the last. It is said that lightning never strikes twice in the same place. Of course, that is not necessarily true. There will be others whom you love that will have to be given up to death.

The callous which developed around the break in my wrist is now like a defensive shield. Never again will that part of my body be as vulnerable as it was at the age of six. In no way is this to say that we should become insensitive to illness or death. It is rather to insist that when living is at its cruelest, and no one escapes those excruciating times, you will be toughened by the heartbreak you are now facing.

"We hear in these days of scientific enlightenment," writes the philosopher, William James, "a great deal of discussion about the efficacy of prayer. Many reasons are given why we should *not* pray. Others give reasons why we *should* pray. Very little is said of the reason we *do* pray."

Multitudes of folks insist they do not believe in prayer. For them it is a useless endeavor. The unexplainable thing is that so many of these same people are seen pleading with some unseen power when their rose colored glasses get smashed. At such a time, we are literally driven to prayer because of the impossibility of the situation. As for *why* we pray, James further observes, "The reason is simple: We pray because we cannot help praying." Abraham Lincoln, during the dark days of the Civil War, remarked, "I have been driven to my knees again and again by the realization that I had nowhere else to go!"

There is no question about it – everyone of us will reach a point where we can no longer neglect prayer. More than likely, that is where you find yourself at this moment. If so . . . turn your eyes heavenward.

Oh God, support us all the day long of this troublous life, until the shadows lengthen and the evening comes, the busy world is hushed, the fever of live is over, and our work is done. Then, in Thy great mercy, grant us a safe lodging and a holy rest, and peace at last. Amen.

DAY 5 . . . DAY BY DAY

Although the human genus is probably the most advanced of all creatures, it is not beneath our dignity to grieve. We share the need to cry with friends in the wild. It is natural to grieve. George Eliot wrote to a friend, "My address is Grief Castle."

Tears are cathartic . . . they tend to cleanse the soul. To hold our hurt inside is to resist the healing of emotions so necessary during bereavement. Crying can be a much-needed therapy. The flippant expression, "Good grief," describes an amazing process by which nature launders our hearts.

There will always be occasions when you will feel the wetness on your cheeks. Let it be. But those moments will come less often than right now. You will never forget. How could you? Why would you want to? The passing of the days, however, are going to dull the ache. That is nature's way of restoring the will to live.

Cooperate with your built-in resistance to defeat. Refuse to surrender your sanity to the demons of defeat. A wise man once said, "There is a time to be born and a time to die . . . . a time to weep and a time to laugh, a time to mourn and a time to dance." It may be too much to ask you to laugh now, but, in time, you must learn to give up the spirit of mourning and dance to the music in your soul – music which will drown out the somber dirge of grief. Melancholy will never go away on its own. But iron-willed discipline will do the job quite well.

DAY BY DAY ... DAY 6

In Egyptian Mythology the day of death is called the "Moment of Initiation into Celestial Life" and the tomb is the 'birthplace.' Cemeteries were called "emerald fields," suggesting intense and living green. Mummy cases had the faces of the deceased painted on them with eyes wide open indicating the occupant was still alive.

Among the peoples of the ancient world none were so sure of immortality as were the Egyptians. The sole purpose of their lives was to prepare for death. The *Book of the Dead* had as its central theme the beautification of the departed. Even the mummy case was referred to as the "chest of the living." A scarab was inserted into the heart cavity as a symbol because, shortly before becoming a pupa, the larva buries itself in the earth from which it emerges a perfect insect. As the sun set, the mummy was ferried over the Lake of Peace to its place of rest in the Land of the Shrouded with the assurance that he would one day meet his loved ones again. Food, raiment and servants were often buried with him to sustain him in his long but rewarding journey.

That was four thousand years ago. But it is a reminder that, from earliest times, the certainty of immortality has pervaded the human mind. Even among the most primitive peoples, the universal cry for more of life underscores the fact that life after death is an intuitive bed-rock of human nature. Why is that gnawing hunger there if not to be satisfied?

DAY 7 ... DAY BY DAY

Mamaw Woodson, as her grandchildren affectionately called her, lived to be ninety-six. In all those years, she never got used to autumn. For her it was a sad time. The leaves were falling, the flowers were fading and the chill of things to come was in the air. Had the family not known it was fall, she would have given the truth away because her mood always changed come September.

It was a little hard for me to understand because autumn is, for me, the most beautiful time of the year. "But, everything is dying," she would say. And I would answer, "Yes, Mom, but look how lovely are the colors!"

If death is anything like October, then it is more glorious than anything we have known as life. Harvest time, with its amber waves of grain; its orange colored moon; its warm, hazy sun – all of it is shot through with a tingling mixture of relaxed excitement. And it is my belief that nothing is more descriptive of death than that.

As the days grow shorter the promise of fall is that we will survive the cruel blasts of winter, our feet toasting by the fire, as we wait the coming of spring when everything we thought was dead bursts from its sodden grave with vigor that declares nothing has died at all. Somewhere I read about a man who, told that he was dying, replied, "This is going to be interesting!" Absolutely. But he could have said, "This is going to be breathtakingly beautiful!"

Jan Struther is gone now, but her beautiful novel, *Mrs. Miniver,* written during World War II will live on forever. At her funeral, a little poem she had written was read. Here is the verse:

> One day my life will end; and lest
> Some whim should prompt you to review it,
> Let her who knew the subject best
> Tell you the shortest way to do it:
> Then say: "Here lies one doubly blest."
> Say: "She was happy." Say: "She knew it."

Most of us, unless we are insufferable egotists, know that life has been good to us, maybe better than we deserved. Right now, you are probably tempted to doubt that. With at least part of your own self lying somewhere in a grave, the easy thing to do is feel sorry for yourself. Wait just a minute. Have you so soon forgotten that it is better to have loved and lost than never to have loved at all?

If the two of you had never met, never established a relationship, you would not be hurting now. Is that the way you wish it had been? Of course not! You wouldn't take a million dollars for the memories. There is no chance that you or your loved one would have been more blessed had your paths never crossed. You had each other – and you still do – forever. Indeed, you have been doubly blest. You surely know it!

DAY 9 ... DAY BY DAY

Some children are afraid of the dark. There may be many reasons for this, but the fundamental one is that they find the darkness untrustworthy. Some adults are afraid of death for the same reason – we distrust eternity. John Dryden was on this wavelength when he scribbled: "Death, in itself, is nothing; but we fear to be we know not what, we know not where."

Since we have no empirical evidence that eternity is as dependable as time, our hearts dread to enter the unknown. Dying, for such people, is a gamble, one which they would avoid if they could. Edmund Blunden, over a hundred years ago, shared man's misgivings when he commented, "Death is the shadow at the door." An even older mystic sang of death as "the valley of the shadow."

The interesting thing is that no one has ever been harmed by a shadow. Facing death is hard because of the shadows, not because of death itself. When C. S. Lewis waded through the murky waters of death with his cherished wife, Joy, he made a discovery which changed his view of death forever. The world to which Joy had gone, the world of shadows, now became a life of substance. The shadows were no longer eternity, but his native England. Hence, Lewis referred to the present state of man as "Shadowlands" in contrast to the substantive reality of heaven. Plato also toyed with the idea when he thought of the earth as nothing more than a poor copy of the real world.

DAY BY DAY . . . DAY 10

If you are like most of us, there are times when you are mad at God. How can a loving God do this to me? Why me and not someone else? Doesn't He know that I trusted Him? These are questions which, if allowed to fester, can make us bitter and resentful.

Have you ever heard anyone say, "Don't ever argue with God"? That is usually pretty good advice, but some of the world's choicest people have done just that. History is replete with biographies of saintly men and women who have vigorously questioned some activity of the divine being. It is never easy to accept something we do not understand.

You have not sinned because you did not agree with God when this happened to you. He does not expect us to be unthinking robots. The sin is not in the argument, but in the bigoted refusal to consider the other side as well as our own. Arguments have a way of resolving themselves if we talk less and listen more. For every word you speak to God today . . . let Him speak ten words to you. You will find that His *unreasonable* ways become quite logical as you learn to listen. True communication with the divine is not monologue – it is dialogue with considerable time in it for thinking.

Anger will eat at your soul like a cancer. It never solves anything. Remember that you do not have all the facts. Your God will never do anything to hurt you. You can trust that.

DAY 11 ... DAY BY DAY

In a very warm moment, Frank L. Stanton, poet laureate of Georgia, wrote a poem for his wife. She cried when she read it, for it spoke of the eternal bond between them. The verse reads like this:

> A little way to walk with you, my own –
> > Only a little way,
> Then one of us must weep and walk alone
> > Until God's day.

> A little way! It is so sweet to live
> > Together, that I know
> Life would not have one withered rose to give
> > If one of us should go.

> And if these lips should ever learn to smile,
> > With thy heart far from mine,
> 'Twould be for joy that in a little while
> > They would be kissed by thine!

To face the death of one we love and yet go on living would be more than could be expected unless we were sure of being together again. It is that inner certainty which keeps us smiling and patiently waiting.

Whether it be the loss of a spouse, a parent, a child, a sibling or a close friend, we all understand the emotion Stanton felt as he contemplated a day of separation. Now that such a day has come, reason demands that we face that "little while" with anticipation of a coming together again.

DAY BY DAY . . . DAY 12

One of the world's most brilliant minds was Albert Einstein, the German born American theoretical physicist. In one of his less guarded moments, he wrote, "Man has no choice in being here. Nor did anyone invite him. He knows not where he is from, neither where he is going, nor why he is here." How I wish he had stayed with his field of physics! With the exception of the first seven words, the whole statement is false.

Unless one subscribes to the shallow theory that all that exists is an unexplainable accident, we are not in the dark about these things. We come from God and return to Him. Then why are we here? We are here to prepare for the return trip. Christopher Morley was wrong, as well, when he said, "Life is a game of whist between man and nature."

Our tenure on earth is one of preparation. Even the early Egyptians knew that. We are sent here for seventy years of schooling. Life is a proving ground, a kind of boot camp, where we toughen and condition ourselves for something bigger and better.

Your Creator has special plans for you today. At the end of this little segment of time, there should be some indication of improvement. To waste one single hour is to subtract from what God wants you to be. Oh yes, we know very well why we are here. The big problem is that we often do not want to acknowledge it. And, in spite of what we are sometimes told, we know where we are going.

DAY 13 ... DAY BY DAY

A recent television advertisement for a cream for chapped, cracked lips claimed that its application provides a 'healing feeling." Whether it works, I do not know. But I do know that a healing feeling is something we all need. In our kind of world – and what other kind is there? – everybody suffers from lots of hurts. Some of us hurt in our bodies, some in our heads and some in our spirits. Often the pain we feel is too much. Physicians, medications and therapy – we try them all, but nothing seems to help.

Are you hurting today? Maybe it's not so much a physical pain as it is a heartache. Do you sometimes feel as if nothing goes right, as if no one cares about you? Is your heart filled with emptiness, as hollow as a bubble stretched so thin it could burst? There is nothing else in the world that hurts like that. But you do not have to keep on hurting. There is an old, oft-proved balm which is still around. It has been here since the beginning. And you cannot believe how different you will feel until you try it.

There are friends out there who are trying to reach you. No matter how they try, the barrier is there. None of us can survive without love. And the tragedy is that, while the world is full of it, some of us insulate ourselves against it. The accepted love of a friend is a healing feeling, a sweet balm which brings comfort and encouragement at the time when it is needed most. Open your arms and your heart and let the healing flow into your weary soul.

When my own wife died, after every known medical treatment had been exhausted, a friend said to me, "We will never know why Gloria had to die, but we do know that she got well."

Passing the aging president, on a street near the capital, a neighbor asked, "How is John Quincy Adams?" To which the venerable old man replied, "Thank you. John Quincy Adams is quite well. But the house where he lives is becoming dilapidated. It is tottering, time and seasons have nearly destroyed it, and it is becoming quite uninhabitable. I shall have to move out soon. But John Quincy Adams is quite well, thank you."

One day you and I will be moving out of this tenement of clay. Already it is in need of repair. As we grow older it is patch on top of patch. The house will not last forever. But the person who lives in it will!

Every cell in your body is sloughed off and replaced with a new one every seven years. Otherwise, the human body would wear out to the point of being discarded at the age of seven. Each time the body wears out, the spirit lives on and continues to thrive, providing itself with a fresh start. Finally, it ceases to rebuild itself. That's what we call death. It is logical to assume that there is still a new dwelling for the spirit of man, a place waiting for us somewhere beyond a flower-strewn mound of earth. The light is on at the end of the tunnel.

DAY 15 . . . DAY BY DAY

On the elevator in the building where I had my office, several persons were descending toward the lobby. As the door opened and one of the riders got off, I said to her, "Have a good day." She made no response. When the door had shut, another lady on the lift turned to me and remarked, "I said that one day to a woman and she replied, "I have already planned my day!"

Have you already planned your day? Is there anyplace in it for a pleasant surprise? Are your days so tightly packed with depression that it would be impossible to have a nice day? If so, unpack them! Give yourself a chance to relax. Allow your rigid mind to unwind. Give yourself a chance to be free from those things which enslave and turn your day into a real disaster. You don't have to end the day with a sigh of relief that it is over. Today can be a joy – a day you will remember – a time you would like to live over again and again.

There is no stress so destructive as that which follows the news of a dear one's death. It is as if a door were slammed in our faces. We feel closed in, unable to move, desperate to breathe. No one else can open the door. The door is locked from within. Even if you have already planned to have a bad day, you can change the course of the next few hours. The decision is up to you. I can wish you a good day a thousand time, but the day will not get better until you want it to, not until you are willing to make it happen.

Never does a day wear to its end without someone's heart being broken. Where there is life, there is also death. Therefore, if death is so universal, you and I need to get a new perspective on it. No way will ever be found that will make it easy to turn loose of our loved ones. They are too much a part of our lives.

Nonetheless, when death is seen aright, the release becomes less a negation and more an affirmation. Helen Frazee-Bower finds a song in the midst of suffering.

There will be music, when the time of grieving
Blots out the stars and darkens all the sky:
Lonely and beautiful, beyond believing,
There will be music – music blowing by.

Out of the darkness it will float and follow,
Closer than arms and kinder than caress:
There will be music filling every hollow
Where grief has made a place for emptiness.

After the tragedies that shake and shatter
The heart's foundation, this will be release –
The sound of music. Nothing else will matter:
There will be music – and a heart at peace.

Were the butterfly, from its lofty flight above, to speak to us, it would point to the dormant pupa on the ground and say, "That is what I once was."

DAY 17 ... DAY BY DAY

"I could not see how the sun could shine when half of my soul lay dead." Those words were spoken by Augustine as he stood, sixteen hundred years ago, beside the grave of his father. That was a long time ago. The passing of the centuries has made it no easier for us to see the sun while looking into the hollow darkness of the grave. There are moments when the awful reality of your loss overpowers the struggle to go on, knocks you flat on your face and defies your effort to get up.

Augustine did see the sun rise again. And his half dead soul refused to die, choosing rather to live and grow. But it did not happen without a will to make it so. Had he not rejected the destructiveness of prolonged grief, there is little question but that the world would not remember his name.

Among history's most influential men and women are those who, with unrequited determination, rose above the heartbreak of loneliness to merge into the traffic of life. To nourish sadness is self-defeating, a kind of mental suicide. The bright flowers of summer will bloom again and they will be more colorful if they are unhampered by weeds. Joy is a flower; sadness is a weed. It is more difficult to get rid of a weed than it is to grow a petunia, but it is worth the effort. Now is a good time to work out your garden. Exterminate the ugliness of sorrow. Feed the beauty of joy. Watch your life blossom again. And, when it does, your soul will awake to the breaking of a brand new morning.

On the occasion of my birthday – one of those decade birthdays which always makes one feel extra old – my children were laughing hysterically as my wife presented me with a beautiful six-foot tall pine tree. Strange birthday gift? Not at all. I had wanted one for a reserved spot in the front yard and that special day was an appropriate time to get it. The day following, I planted that little tree with the help of my laughing children. Since I was growing older it was a symbol of my immortality. A young monk once said, "If I knew I would die tomorrow, I would plant a tree today." He must have been feeling what I felt.

Birthdays are cherished by children and dreaded by the rest of us. That ought not be the case. Our heats should be filled with thanksgiving as we celebrate – yes, *celebrate* – growing older. Getting older is not synonymous with quitting. There are still a lot of living and loving things you can do. Bake a loaf of bread for a neighbor. Take somebody who has no car on a shopping spree. Put on your best suit and take a walk. Smile at passing people. Give a dollar to a kid. Take someone with you to church.

Even if you are still young you will feel old if you give in to the passing years. Living without that somebody can make you feel very, very old. Refuse to let these tough times conquer you. Whether you have only a few years left or more than you can imagine, celebrate what is left. Do something today which will outlive you. That's why I planted a tree.

DAY 19 . . . DAY BY DAY

Once life has knocked the breath out of us, it may be enough to make us afraid to breathe again. What are you afraid of today? The lion, which Dorothy meets in *The Wizard Of Oz,* roars and brags about being the king of the jungle when, in reality, he is a big pussy-cat. When he finally meets the wizard in person and asks for some courage, the great one rolls on the ground in laughter. The very idea – the king of the jungle with no courage! But the lion timidly explains that he has no courage "only when I'm scared." That's not hard to understand, is it? When I am not scared I have plenty of courage. But when I am really scared – that's when I want to hide.

The commanding officer asked a soldier, who bragged about his bravery, why he was such a coward in conflict. He replied, "Sir, I have a heart as brave as Julius Caesar, but when the enemy is mentioned, my feet run away with my heart." Just living in the world demands a good dose of courage. Life is not always kind. Everybody, with no exception, has a share in adversity. There are times when our plans literally explode in our faces. That's when we really get scared.

That which has so recently happened to you has left your life in shreds, the breath knocked out of you. You are trying to catch your breath but it is so hard to pull yourself together and try again. You must not run away from life. Stay and fight! Tell your feet to behave. Don't run away, but listen to your heart.

No one is dead until his work is done. It is not possible that man can do immortal things and not be himself immortal! We know that death does not end it all because when we approach the grave we feel, as Victor Hugo, that we have done but a tiny bit of what is in us. The soul inherently reaches out for life and we may be sure that the Creator, who invested us with this grasp, will honor it at last. Among Robert Browning's last words were, "Never say that I am dead!" There is still music in us after we have breathed our last.

Love demands a future life. Even where there is no religion, there is love. The philosopher, David Hume, skeptic that he was, confesses that when he thought of his mother he believed in immortality.

It may be properly said that man is in exile, away from his native land. At the moment he is permitted to return, he flies back to God. Divinity is ingrained within us and we are never satisfied with our humanity. Hugo insists that every man hears the symphonies of the world toward which he moves. Perhaps this is what Augustine had in mind when he suggested man is made for God and cannot find rest until he finds it there. The homing call is so much a part of our makeup that only a few can live out their allotted days without a longing for their origin and their destination . . . they are really one and the same. Death then can be a coming home after a long and harrowing journey through a far away land.

DAY 21 . . . DAY BY DAY

The old Bruton Parish Church, in colonial Williamsburg, dates back to the days of George Washington and Thomas Jefferson. Actually, the present building was erected between 1711 and 1715 and has been in constant use as a place of worship until this present day. In the churchyard, one finds numerous tombs with crumbling stones marking the resting place of many of the men and women who helped procure our independence from England. One is hushed while walking in the musty air of the old burial grounds. Many stories of bravery and love could be told if those monuments could speak.

Someday everyone of us will be stretched beneath the earth in some similar place. Perhaps three hundred years hence people will be reading our markers and remembering something we did. Hopefully, as they listen to the voice of the stones, they will hear some heroic story of love and courage. What have you done that you would want retold by those granite sentinels? Is there anything you would want kept a secret? The life you and I live today determines the message we leave.

A simple epitaph chiseled into granite over a woman's grave in a country cemetery tells us a lot about her life. It reads: "She hath done what she could." The one thing that you could do right now is to stand tall and straight, confronting your sorrow with resolute determination. Never let anyone remember you as one who failed to do what you could!

Years ago airplane propellers were made of wood from trees on the islands which had endured the resistance of hurricanes without breaking. Revolving on a power driven shaft at hundreds of miles per hour, propellers had to be tough as nails.

"Life is a grindstone and whether it grinds a man down or polishes him up depends on what he is made of." Whoever wrote those words did not sign his name, but the anonymity does not make them any less true. Living does have a way of being abrasive. We sometimes refer to our days as "the grind."

All of us know what happens when we put coffee or pepper in a mill. It is reduced to small granules, sometimes powder. But, if we put a diamond in there, it is a different story. A grinding stone wears down everything except a diamond; the diamond wears down the stone.

How tough are you? Can you take it? I do not mean to be insensitive, but when the day is over do you feel like a victor or a victim? It all depends on the kind of stuff from which you are made. I believe that you are tough enough to stand up to the most severe abuse. He who created you made you from His best material. People are God's diamonds – in the rough, of course – but diamonds nevertheless. There is nothing tougher in the world. The grief that defies you today is no match for the conquering power of the human mind. With the help of God and your friends, you can wear down the grindstone!

DAY 23 ... DAY BY DAY

Is there any greater miracle than that which takes place when a farmer drops a grain of corn in the ploughed soil? One would be hard pressed to think of anything more incredibly amazing. Yet, it has been going on so long that hardly any of us gives it a thought.

That grain of corn, from all appearances, has no future. It is dry and hard as a rock . . . the kind of thing which might be used to pave a road. But bury it in the ground and stand back! There it will die and live again, bursting through the earth with unbelievable vigor. And it will outdo itself, becoming more luxurious than ever before. A life like that is worth dying for.

What kind of logic would argue that what happens to a grain of corn is to be expected, but nothing similar could ever happen to a man? Seed, which have been left uncovered for thousands of years, have been planted with the startling results of watching them grow. Could there be more life power in a grain of corn than in a human being?

It would help if there were an observer as much greater than man as a man is greater than corn, but there isn't. Or is there? From the outset of the human race, it has been a sneaking suspicion that Someone is watching. But observing from His perspective, it is likely that our Creator's view is much enlarged. Might that not be why we are endowed with the idea that man is as immortal as corn?

DAY BY DAY ... DAY 24

Looking at life can be rewarding or it can be defeating. It all depends on what you want to see. Negative folks see one thing: positive people see another. Looking back everything is full of shadows, but looking forward everything is filled with sunshine.

One morning a ninety-seven year old man walked into an insurance office and asked to take out a policy on his life. The agent pushed an application across the counter. When the agent noted the man's age on the application he explained that no one could sell him insurance at that age. "You people are making a big mistake," replied the old man. "If you look over your statistics, you'll discover that mighty few men die after they are ninety-seven."

It all depends on how you look at it, doesn't it? Is the glass half-full of water or half-empty? How do you look at life now that you have gone through this earth-shattering experience? Is life filled with problems you can't get around or is it full of unlimited possibilities? Does the future present only dark images of failure or does it convey bright visions of success? Are you lucky to be alive or do you think of continuing to live as an unfortunate predicament? Was the man ninety-seven years old or ninety-seven years young? Is life all over or could I sign a new lease on life?

These are all questions which probe our souls. Answering them correctly could mean the difference between life and death. Look at life through gray glasses. What do you see? Now try pink ones!

DAY 25 . . . DAY BY DAY

A Line from the stage production, *Pump Boys and Dinettes*, "Worry is like a rocking chair. It gives you something to do, but it doesn't get you anywhere." That is true. But it is also a fact that worry is unlike a rocking chair in that rocking can be a pleasant pastime while worry is a miserable pursuit, Occasionally, one is seen rocking as if he were going to a fire. But *all* worriers work at the business of worrying as if they were paid for it.

Worry is the most useless thing in the world. At least rocking in a good chair brings some relaxation after a hard day's work. Worry only adds to the tension, and we all have more tension than we need.

Ultimately, it must be agreed that undue worry is a dead give-a-way that we do not trust life. When Henry Ford was asked if he ever worried, he said, "No, I believe God is managing affairs and that He doesn't need any advice from me. With God in charge, I believe that everything will work out for the best in the end. So what is there to worry about?" Good question: What is there to worry about?

Unless we have faith in the future, there will be little going on in our lives. We won't drive a car. We won't build a house. We won't even eat our dinner. Confidence is the first step to getting on with your life. If you wait for moving on until everything is under your personal supervision, you will finally stop breathing altogether. Without trust you will sit in the corner of your room and rock your life away.

DAY BY DAY ... DAY 26

She was only thirty-nine. As she lay dying, comatose to all around her, we heard her murmur in delight: "Oh, my beautiful home! My beautiful home!" And those of us who loved her knew her remarks were not reflective, but anticipatory.

Thomas Wolfe, in *Can't Go Home Again*, muses: "Someone has spoken to me in the night – and told me I shall die, I know not where. Saying: to lose the life you have, for greater life; to leave the friends you loved, for greater loving; to find a land more kind than here, more large than earth."

Ashley was five years old. Enamored by the covered bridge which crossed the creek to our house, she stared at the little marker over the arch which read: *Entrance.* In deep concentration, she asked, "Is the other side the *outrance?* You and I are not in a primeval forest, lost in a maze of darkness. We are in transit; we are going somewhere. If birth is an entrance, then death is an outrance from this world, but an entrance to the bright world on the other side.

Philip of Macedon, father of Alexander the Great, ordered his counselor to enter the royal courts every morning and say: "Philip! Philip! Remember that thou must die!" He needed also to be reminded, "Philip! Philip! Remember that thou must live!"

It may be easier to dwell on thoughts of death, at the moment, than those of life. But dying will take care of itself if you work on living.

DAY 27 . . . DAY BY DAY

One afternoon, during a World Series game in Chicago, the renowned Babe Ruth stepped to the plate and pointed to the distant ball park fence. The fans knew, without his saying a word, that he was planning to knock the ball over it. As the third pitch came across the plate, Babe swung and over the fence went the ball. The crowd nearly tore down the grandstand in excitement. Later, a reporter asked Ruth what he would have done if he had missed the third strike. And, without hesitation, he replied, "I never thought about it!"

That's what you call positive thinking. Babe Ruth never once entertained the thought that he might strike out. And so he didn't. Most of us strike out in life, not because we are bad hitters, but because we keep convincing ourselves that it might happen. It is astounding how much a poor attitude can adversely affect what we are able to do. Just keep on thinking that you are going to fail and you will. No one wins at anything unless he is so sure of the outcome that he gives it all he has got. The more doubtful we are about the future, the more certain is disaster.

Negative thinking has failure built into it from the beginning. Don't think about striking out today. That's for other people . . . not you! You are standing at the plate right now. The ball is being pitched to you. This is your chance. What will you do with it? Will you swing and miss? Or will you knock the ball out of the park? It's up to you.

Marcus Annius Verus was born in Rome in 121 A.D. He was given the name Marcus Aurelius by the Roman emperor who adopted him. In 161 he succeeded his adoptive father to the throne and ruled until his death in 180. Commenting on his death, in his *Meditations,* he says, "Thou hast embarked, thou hast made the voyage, thou art come to shore; get out." While these words come across as somewhat callous to those of us who are sensitive to the trauma of dying, they offer sober advice that loses its harshness once we recover from the shock.

Life here is an adventure exactly like all lesser voyages – it has a destination. When one reaches that "far distant shore" there should be no hesitancy as to what to do. Arrival is what we had in mind, from the outset, and to reject the end of the journey is to cancel the importance of the whole trip.

He had been through a battery of tests as he waited for the lab report. Shaking his head and speaking softly, the doctor said, "Not good news, George. You have three months to live. I am sorry." Reaching for the hand of his physician, the man who had just received his death sentence, replied, "Don't be sorry, doctor. This is what I've been living for!"

There is no reason for anyone to draw back from death. Do not deny your loved one the joy of fulfillment. As always, once we arrive at our destination, we simply *get out,* walk ashore and commence a new adventure.

DAY 29 . . . DAY BY DAY

Sometimes it is hard to understand the way life treats us. Jack Benny once said, as he received an sward for his illustrious work as a comedian, "I don't deserve this award, but I have arthritis and I don't deserve that either."

So often life appears to play mean tricks on us. The promotion we expected at work doesn't come through. Our children do not turn out like we had hoped. The dreams we shared with the family do not come true. Lingering illness knocks us off our feet. A loved one is taken for no apparent reason. Everything bad that could happen . . . happens. And we cry out in despair, "I don't deserve this!"

That is probably right. Most of the time people do not deserve the bad things. No one has an answer as to why this is so. But, then, none of us deserves the good things either! And how often has life poured out good things upon us when we least expected them? The trouble is that we always think we deserve everything good, but nothing bad. We are so spoiled and pampered that we argue against accepting our share of the world's hard knocks. It is one thing to watch the neighbor up the street suffer. But it is another thing when that suffering invades *our* warm and cozy homes. Somehow it is just unfair!

Be grateful for the blessings life gives you. Count your many blessings . . . they will surprise you. If one had a way of knowing, the good always outweighs the bad.

One of the laughter-inducing commercials on television recently was that of an express delivery service. This fellow, sold on his company, answers the phone and responds to two or three customers making hard requests, "I can do that; I can do that; I can do that." Then, as he hangs up the phone, with a puzzled look he says to himself, *"How* am I going to do that?"

There are times when we get ourselves into trouble by promising too much. But there are other times when we do not expect enough of ourselves. We are sure of only one thing . . . I can't do that! And if that is the way we think – then we can't. *Can* and *cannot* are separated only by personal resolve.

Life throws some pretty tough things at us and, unless we are ready, we will sit down and give up. The stress becomes so heavy that we think we are going to smother beneath the avalanche. What we have to do when we feel like saying, "I can't do that," is start talking seriously to ourselves. Say, "Yes you can; yes you can; yes you can . . ." Say it over and again until you drown out those crippling thoughts.

What is the one thing you would like to do most today? Whatever it is, there is no reason why you cannot do it. The difficult things take a little honest effort and the impossible things require a bit more. You can do whatever you want to do if you want to do it badly enough. Muster your will. No matter how hard it is just keep saying "Yes I can!" and you will. I am going to be rooting for you.

DAY 31 ... DAY BY DAY

I like the instruction Robert Louis Stevenson gave to his family before his untimely death in 1894.

> This be the verse you grave for me:
> Here he lies where he longed to be;
> Home is the sailor, home from the sea,
> And the hunter home from the hill.

From time immemorial, man has reckoned, in his saner moments, that death is not the monster of greed we have been made to believe. It is not as if some grim reaper cuts us down, clapping his filthy hands in glee. The moment of dying may be the most pleasant one has ever enjoyed. "How beautiful is Death," penned the poet Shelley, "Death and his brother Sleep." Yet, lest life be meaningless, dying has to be more than endless sleep.

In autumn, when everything appears to be dying, one might think of nature as being asleep. But the spring rains come and the sun bursts across the earth and mother nature wipes the sleep from her eyes. While the grave may rightly be thought of in terms of sleep, it is frightening to think that the one we love might never wake again. Around the world, the cherished hope is the same, the hope that life goes on. For most of us, it is much more than hope. It is faith. Death then, must be seen more as a much deserved rest than as a long sleep.

The cash register rings in the department store; the morning traffic rolls on at breakneck speed; the club house is filled with laughing people; the sports area resounds with the yelling of jubilant fans – but it is not for you. "The world rushes on over the strings of the lingering heart," wrote Tagore, the Indian poet, "making the music of sadness." And you wonder how life can go on.

The world has stopped turning. It is all over. Nothing is left but a dirge in the night, the *music of sadness*. Looking at the bustling world outside your window, through eyes glazed with tears, everything you see is a dull blur. No doubt about it . . . nothing will ever be the same again. That's the way you feel today.

How could the person I loved most in the world do this to me? Do not be surprised if such a thought enters your mind because it is not unusual to feel rejected by the one who has died, as if he or she wanted to get away. With feelings of rejection come feelings of quilt: What could I have done differently? Where did I go wrong? Did I fail to show enough love? It's all my fault. I should have been a better husband, a more supportive wife, a more understanding parent, a more responsible child, a more dependable friend.

Self-flagellation isn't going to help. Should one want to get away there is a number of better ways of doing it than by dying. Put the whip away. Stop lashing out at yourself for something you did not do and cannot control.

DAY 33 . . . DAY BY DAY

Her husband of many years lay dead before our empty stares. The room was silent, the quiet broken only by muffled whispers. Then, loudly enough for all to hear, from behind her tears came the unexpected words, "He deserved to die."

Sadly, you and I have been led to believe that, if one is bad enough, he deserves to die. But death is not punishment. She was speaking of a good man, a loving husband, a giant among his peers. For him, who had lived and loved so well, death was the grandest thing that could happen! He deserved to die.

In light of such a statement, one might say that a funeral should be seen as celebration. The ancient Chinese proverb, "Weep at a birth and laugh at death" declares life after death to be an improvement over life after birth.

To expect us to divest ourselves of sorrowful weeping at the departure of a loved one is more than can be asked. It hurts when we face separation from those who have been such a vital part of our lives. We never want to give them up even when they express a desire to go. But our reluctance to let go must be seen as the selfishness which it is. Emotions are mixed, of course, but most of our weeping comes from thoughts of what their leaving will mean to us. Admittedly, it would never be appropriate to weep over what they are going to gain. They deserve it. And we would do better to rejoice with them than to mourn for ourselves.

Following his defeat of Napoleon III, in the Franco-Prussian War, Otto von Bismarck was made imperial chancellor and prince of Germany, a position where he remained until the accession of Kaiser Wilhelm II. In a discussion about immortality with Andrew White, America's ambassador to Germany, the prince said, "I do not doubt it, even for a moment. This life is too sad, too incomplete, to satisfy our highest aspirations and desires. It is meant to be a struggle to ennoble us. Can the struggle be in vain? I think not. Final perfection, I believe in, a perfection which God has in store for us."

Within each of us resides the conviction that death short-circuits our possibilities. Accepting the fact that our work is done here, there yet remains the unfulfilled desire to do something more. Michelangelo is now working on his masterpiece. Beethoven must be writing symphonies somewhere. Byron's poetry flows from his finger tips in a perfection he never knew on earth. The plays of Shakespeare have reached a maturity not possible until now.

Out souls possess too much potential for this world alone. We need more time. The energy inside us must be released to continue its work. How that comes about we do not know, but that it does we are certain. That has been the instinct of every person who ever lived. Neither cynicism nor skepticism from critics of our determination to continue have ever been able to frustrate that universal hope.

DAY 35 . . . DAY BY DAY

In our yard stand several elm trees. They are large and tall and one of them is very old. Every time there is a wind or a little too much snow, some of the bigger limbs come crashing to the ground. Now there are also willow trees growing down by the edge of the creek, which go through the snows and the storms without a fracture. The difference, you see, is that one tree will bend while the other will not.

Our days are not always calm and sunny. The winds blow, the snows fall, and the storms beat furiously upon us. Unless we learn how to bend a little we will break up and go to pieces. When this happens we call it a *nervous breakdown.*

People who come through the hard times, without being torn to shreds, are those who learn to lean with the punches. As long as we are afraid of life there is not a chance, in the world, that we will release the tension on our nerves. Apprehension and anxiety wreak their havoc in the smallest storms.

When the big storms come, like that you are going through at the moment, one has to be doubly flexible. The stiffer we stand in defiance of the wind, the more damage it will do. It is at times like this that each of us has to cooperate with nature. Having bucked the storms before, we think we are awfully tough, but the best thing to do now is to relax and bend a little. You are in the hands of something or Someone more powerful than any one of us, and it will help to remember that nature is not against us.

The other day I saw, in the back window of a car in the lane in front of me, a picture of Garfield the cat with the words, "I don't Love anybody!" There are people like that. They are so miserable with life that there is nothing to like and no one to love. And it is always their own fault. If we are to be happy, we must be loved. And if we are to be loved, we must love somebody. Love is not something we say, it is something we do . . . and something we are. How sad to be a nobody.

Feeling and expressing love for others is the surest way to avoid loneliness. It is true that to love is to be vulnerable. Sometimes people who love get hurt. But it is far better to hurt with love in your heart than it is to hurt without it.

Love is a cushion which mellows and softens the hard blows we all must face. Without love, the world is too much for us. We succumb to its loveless ways when we permit love to die within us.

When we lose the person we loved the most it may be hard to love again at all. In our grief, we expect others to reach out to us in love. Lest we forget . . . we who are lonely must reach out in love ourselves. I hope you are not thinking, "I don't love anybody." Nobody likes a Garfield complex. Such an attitude will destroy you. Find someone – to whom you may give your love. Give it unstintedly and it will come back to you a thousand fold for sharing is receiving.

DAY 37 . . . DAY BY DAY

Will, speaking at Mr. O'Hara's funeral in *Gone With the Wind* by Margaret Mitchell, says "There warn't nothin' that come to him from the outside that could lick him . . . . But he had our failin's too, 'cause he could be licked from the inside. I mean to say that what the whole world couldn't do, his own heart could . . . . And I want to say this – folks whose mainsprings are busted are better dead."

When inner resolve is gone, there is very little left. There is nothing unusual about the death of a person who has lost the will to live. Many of us are dead while we live because we have no conviction or commitment to life. When that takes place we have given up on being anything more than a person who eats his bread and goes to bed.

As long as one has the inner will to really live, to contribute something to the world around him, to make a difference because he is here – there is nothing outside that person which can lick him. On the other hand, without that will, any one of us will fold his tent long before he needs to.

For some people, the death of a family member or a special friend is total defeat. No more conquests, no more victories . . . just resignation to defeat. The mainspring is usually not broken, just allowed to run down and never be wound again. Has the spring gone from your step? Has the fire in your heart gone out? Fan the sparks on the hearth. Let your heart blaze again. You have no right to die before your time.

DAY BY DAY . . . DAY 38

A *master of English prose* was the seventeenth century Richard Baxter. At the end of his most famous work is this beautiful passage in which he describes one's view as he enters the portals of death.

"Thou wilt be as one that stands on the top of an exceeding high mountain; he looks down on the world as if it were quite below him; fields and woods, cities and towns, seem to him as but little spots. Thus despicably wilt thou look on all things here below. The greatest princes will seem as grasshoppers; the busy, contentious, covetous world, but as a heap of ants. Man's threatenings will be no terror to thee; nor the honours of this world any strong enticement; temptations will be more harmless, as having lost their sting; and every mercy will be better known and relished."

If we could see into the life beyond there is every reason to believe that the surprise would be more than the human mind can conceive. Nathaniel Hawthorne once observed, "We sometimes congratulate ourselves at the moment of waking from a troubled dread; it may be so the moment after death."

It is because we know so little about the details of life after death that some dread it. By the same token, it is the reason why others of us await it with joyful anticipation. The little which our inner spirits hint should be enough to whet our appetites for the real thing. But before we can look down from the mountain top we must climb the heights themselves.

DAY 39 . . . DAY BY DAY

I have never seen a man or woman who did not believe in immortality when standing by the open grave. No one can look upon the still form of another and not remember the intellect and love, as well as the vast faculties of energy which animated that cold body, and say, "I have buried my wife; I have buried my child; I have buried my sister . . . forever." As we turn from the mournful lowering of the coffin and the gut-wrenching tossing of the earth, we never fail to hear the all but inaudible sound of angel wings.

When you stretch out your hands to God, eyes brimming with salty tears, it is not enough to believe that He turns away, consigning our hopes to a yawning grave, mocking our plea for more of life. Such would be contrary to the nature of God or, as some would put it, to the God of nature."

At the funeral of his brother, Robert G. Ingersol, an avowed infidel, spoke with deliberate words: "Life is a narrow vale between the cold and barren peaks of two eternities. We strive in vain to look beyond the height. We cry aloud – and the only murmur is the echo of our wailing cry. From the voiceless lips of the un-replying Dead there comes no word. But in the night of Death, Hope sees a star, and listening can hear the rustling of a wing."

Or, as Victor Hugo so emphatically expressed it: "The nearer I approach the end the plainer I hear around me the immortal symphonies of the world which invite me."

DAY BY DAY ... DAY 40

Affectionately remembered as "The Hoosier Poet," James Whitcomb Riley continues to warm our hearts with his dialectal verse. Often his words are read, after a hundred years, with comforting effect at memorial services across the land.

> I can't say, and I will not say
> That he is dead. He is just away.
>
> With a cheery smile and a wave of the hand,
> He has wandered into an unknown land
>
> And left us dreaming how very fair
> I needs must be, since he lingers there.
>
> And you – oh, you, who the wildest yearns
> For an old-time step, and a glad return,
>
> Think of him faring on, as dear
> In the love of There as the love of Here.
>
> Think of him still as the same. I say
> He is not dead – he is just away.

Johann Wolfgang von Goethe never flinched in the presence of death. "I am fully convinced," he said, "that the soul is indestructible, and that its activities will continue through eternity. It is like the sun, which, to our eyes seems to set at night; but it has really gone to diffuse its light elsewhere." Such is the conclusion of wisdom.

DAY 41 . . . DAY BY DAY

   This is not the time to stop living. You may think it is, but nothing could be further from the truth. About the only contribution your departed loved one can now make to the world is the encouragement to continue with life. But you can become the glove on the hand of the one who is so greatly missed, the instrument with which one in another world can carry on in a land where he is no longer seen.

   Your charge is now greatly enlarged. Now you are called upon to live for two, not just one. It may be that you must now be both father and mother to your children. Or you may have to pursue some labor which meant more than anything else to the one now gone from the workbench. Although that interest may have been nothing more than keeping weeds out of a manicured garden, if it was important to him or her, you must carry on. Did he volunteer at the hospital? You can do that for him. Did she send cards to others in distress? Now is the time for you to take up the pen and do what your loved ones would do were they still here. In this way their works will follow them.

   By working at the things your loved one believed important, you are adding years to his or her life. The best way to handle loneliness is by keeping busy. So, forget about quitting! The work is already piling up. Living for two will demand a lot from you, but the joy of knowing the one you love is still your partner will be its own reward.

DAY BY DAY . . . **DAY 42**

Still mad at God, are you? Our youngest daughter, about four years old at the time, was playing by herself, in the dirt, outside the kitchen window. Hearing her arguing loudly with someone who was nowhere to be seen, her mother raised the window and asked, "Who are you fussing at?" "God!" came the frustrated reply of a little girl frantically grabbing at her playthings. "And why are you mad at God?" With mounting disgust in her voice, she replied, "Because He won't keep his wind away from my pies!"

Being a lot older than four does not make us less apt to vent our anger on God for the bad things that happen to good people like ourselves. Who among us does not do that sometimes? Life can become so frustrating for us that we just have to lash out at somebody. God is always our nearest neighbor so He catches it. Man's ever present scapegoat is He who takes it on the chin again and again with no vocal defense. All of us find it easy to lay the blame for anything irritating on the One who is bound to be responsible when things go wrong.

The emotion of anger and clenched-fist resistance is understandable. But blaming God is a cop out. May I suggest that, instead of foolishly holding Someone accountable, you might try thanking Him for the irritating moments that will ultimately increase your stamina for living. Temper your response to the bitter winds that blow over your days. Any other reaction to adversity will only fester in your heart.

DAY 43 . . . DAY BY DAY

From the halls of anonymity comes the classic verse of a poor sharecropper, a wise and sensitive man of the earth who learned to be thankful in spite of the bad stuff.

> Good Lawd sends me troubles,
>   And I got to wuk 'em out.
> But I look aroun' an' see
>   There's trouble all about.
> An ' when I see my troubles
>   I jes' look up an' grin
> To think ob all de troubles
>   Dat I ain't in!

Helen Adams Keller was deaf and blind from infancy. Yet she often remarked, "Keep your face to the sunshine and you cannot see the shadows," Sunshine for Helen was not an orange ball of fire in the sky – that she had never seen – but rather happy thoughts, laughing people and beautiful memories. Try walking in that kind of sunshine today and the somber shadows will always fall behind you.

Magnifying our problems is a trait common to mankind. But concentrating on our troubles only breeds more trouble. If the soul is dyed the color of its thoughts, we have our first insight into why some folks find life so dreary. Sorrow's ruts wear deeper and deeper. Soon they are so entrenched that there is no way out. Climb out while you can. Face the sunshine and think of all the trouble you ain't in!

When you and I first started this pilgrimage together we agreed – if not in a verbal contract, at least in spirit – to face the grim reality of death one day at a time. Today we are having our mid-term exam. The only question is how you are doing with your part of the agreement. Even during periods of joy and gladness some of us have trouble with the past or the future . . . or both. The past either haunts us with memories of experiences better forgotten or it makes us sad remembering the good time. And the future? Well, we dread it like the plague or we find ourselves plunging head first before we are ready. And the present becomes little more than an unused bridge between where we've been and where we are going.

The most important day in your life is today. The past is gone and will never return. The future is not here yet and may never arrive. But you are smack in the middle of today. It would be a pity to lose it.

Fearing to go forward and wishing to go back is to lose sight of the fact that today is the tomorrow you worried about yesterday, the day you will wish you could get back when it is gone. Live today . . . it's all you have. People who re-live the past or pre-live the future are wasting the one day they can really call their own. Do not spend you life on broken dreams, bits and pieces of nostalgia or speculation. Squeeze as much life into today as you can. Once it is gone, it is gone forever, but as long as it is here it is yours to do with as you will. Don't overlook it.

DAY 45 ... DAY BY DAY

Happiness is a shy nymph who runs away when we try to woo her. She is already wed to so many things that to seek her without her companions is to fail in our pursuit. Happiness is a by-product which appears when we have somebody to love, something to do and something to look forward to. I hope you have someone to love and someone to love you in return – a spouse, a child, an aunt, a friend. Life is pretty rotten without love. I also hope that you have something to do, some worthy job to perform, some project to complete. Work and the satisfaction one feels in its accomplishment is an indispensable requirement for happiness. But even if you have love and a job, you must have hope for the future or you have nothing at all.

How does your future look right now? Does it have promise or is it a blur? Recently, I heard a man say he had no interest in what happens after he dies. Impossible! Everybody is interested in the ultimate future. We can talk pretty tough as if it were weakness to hope, but living with no hope that the best is yet to be is a hole in a doughnut. I'm thankful for those who love me and for a task to perform. Life wouldn't be much without that. But I am most thankful that life is going to get better until it becomes the best of all.

Happiness is not dependent on everything going well. It is rather that shy nymph who comes when circumstances may be at their worst, but when hope and her wiser sister, faith, are at their best.

Immortality is on everyone's mind, believer and cynic alike. One of the most striking comments ever made on the subject was that of Hortense, daughter of Napoleon's Josephine and mother of Napoleon III. His son, seriously ill in America, was reported to be near death. In a letter to him, she wrote, "Believe that certainly we shall meet again. Have faith in this consoling idea. It is too necessary not to be true."

At the bedside of his dying daughter, Louis Pasteur was heard to say, "I know only scientifically determined truth, but I am going to believe what I wish to believe, what I cannot help but believe – I expect to meet this dear child in another world."

For many years, it has been tradition to wear black or dark clothing at funerals. Black bands are yet seen on arms of people who are remembering a deceased friend. But Ruskin asks a viable question: "Why should we wear black for the quests of God?" Dark and somber thoughts must not color our attitudes about death. None of us would think of wearing black because a friend goes on an extended vacation. Of course, that is because we expect to see them again. Death is a morbid and ghastly thing if we cannot see through the cypress trees. It may safely be said that the grandest thought ever to enter the human mind is the hope of immortality. Thus, we relinquish our loved ones, for a while, with the inner assurance that we shall one day be together again.

DAY 47 . . . DAY BY DAY

The comedy actor, Danny Kaye, once said, "Life is a great big canvas, and you should throw all the paint on it you can." Amateurs though we may be, every man, woman and child is painting a picture called *Life.* No, we do not have pallette and brush or oils and tints, but we nonetheless are working on what will one day become a masterpiece or a thing of terrible embarrassment. Some think they can spend their days without producing a picture at all, but that is not true. The canvas will not remain empty. It may be splotched with blacks and bleak grays, or it may be resplendent with a variety of bright colors. There will be something on the canvas when we are finished.

Life should be a celebration. Throw all the paint you can. Life is beautiful and it ought to be a highland fling. There is nothing drab about it. It should sing and dance like a bubbling teapot. In the event your own life is like a lead balloon . . . get the lead out! Use your wings. Why crawl when you can soar? A person without a vibrant spirit is like a hot air balloon with no fire. Look at the canvas again. Erase the gloom. Splash it with all the color you can give. There is nothing dull about living.

Danny Kaye was not being funny. He was dead serious . . . and he was absolutely correct. The great Michelangelo may have been able to paint the ceiling of the Sistine Chapel lying on his back. But you and I are not so good. We have to get back on our feet and address the canvas with a vengeance.

DAY BY DAY ... DAY 48

That we should survive death is not to me an incredible thing at all. The thing which defies logic is why the existence of Life at all. How am I to understand the appearance of life on this particular planet? Where can I find rationale for this world of stars? Why are you here? Why am I? How do we explain the sun in the sky, the source of life and energy for this distant planet? Why is the grass green, the sky blue, the atmosphere filled with oxygen? Did all this just happen? By Chance? All this designed orderliness and beauty – just blind chance? Who are we kidding?

Something must have started the whole thing. First, there was nothing ... then there was something. That's what is incredible. For something to come out of nothing demands energy beyond the presence of Life itself, a power prior to and greater than Life. We have been called out of the unknown. Our wills had nothing to do with it. Man did not make himself.

Nothing could be more unreasonable than to assume there was nothing before the universe unless it is the assumption that there is nothing after it! The same God who called us out of the mystery of the past now calls us into the mystery of the future. He who designed this world for man has simply created a like world for man's continuance. It would be as mentally irresponsible to deny a God who restores us as to deny a God who created us. The big mystery is not that man shall be, but that man is. If the latter is true the former must follow as truth also.

DAY 49 . . . DAY BY DAY

The sun was blistering but the garden danced with delight. I was looking at the beautiful flowers and shrubs which a sixty-five year old man had planted on the steep bank in his front yard. He was noticeably proud of his work completed with a bad back and under a hot sky. His shirt was wet and sweat dripped from his nose and chin. Wiping his face with an old bandana, he turned toward me and said, "I told my wife that we are just doing this for someone else to enjoy." I could see he was flustered more by what he had said than by the strain in his back. Of course, he was lamenting the possibility that he might not be around long to enjoy what he had done.

In all my years, I have never met a person who did not want perpetuity. We want to be assured that we are going to be good for something more than seventy years and that what we do will live after us. If that is what we want, there is something we can do which will insure it.

Do something that will outlive you, something good. The world does not easily forget those who leave their mark so deeply etched by good works that others find it impossible to ignore. Spend your days in service to your family, your friends and to neighbors whose names you may not even know. One's life is authenticated by the enduring work he does, by the selfless contribution she makes. The best way in the world to fight your own loneliness is by doing something good for someone else.

DAY BY DAY . . . DAY 50

From the legends of an earlier day, comes a story about a child being comforted by a holy man following the death of the boy's dog. Numb with grief, the boy listened as the holy man explained why the pet did not just disappear, but remained visible at the child's feet. The whole thing was nature's way of teaching a lesson about another world.

Handing a small shell, from the sea shore, to the weeping child, the wise teacher explained that the tiny creature, which had lived in this house, had departed. "Now watch the shell and listen," he told the boy, lifting his little chin so that he could look into the eyes of his teacher. As the boy listened to the shell's story of the sea, the hurt in his heart began to heal. He learned that a house could be discarded while the creature that lived in it continued to live somewhere else.

It is God's plan that everything in the experience of boys and girls – and especially grown up ones – must undergo change. Your loved ones will be taken from you if you live long enough. Only recently have you learned that lesson and the sadness refuses to go away. Look again at that empty shell. If creatures, who leave their shells, continue to live beyond the bounds of their earlier restrictive houses, surely it is reasonable to believe that men and women continue to live somewhere else after discarding their old, worn out houses of flesh. Even a boy, who has lost his puppy, understands that.

DAY 51 . . . DAY BY DAY

Let your heart be filled with gladness that you were given the time you shared with the one you loved so much. Think about the good times, the strolls down lover's lane, the drives in the country, the picnic in the park, the shared pride when junior stumbles over his words in the school play. Think about the coming of children and grandchildren, the tough times and the good, the little things that made memories.

Granny stood at the open door of the Greyhound bus, her eyes running with tears, as she pulled little Jimmy to her breast and kissed his curly head. He had spent most of the summer at his grandparents' house in the country. The driver had made his last call to the passengers and Jimmy was pulling away from his grandmother. She was sobbing now, loathe to turn loose. With a final big hug, little Jimmy said. "Don't be sad because I'm leaving, Granny. Be happy that I came!"

Of course, this is a sad time for you. Someone has left and you did not want that special person to go. Had you been permitted to make a choice, you would have stayed together forever. Now you are wallowing in your sadness when you could be basking in how wonderful it all has been. Too much crying can blind us to the happiness that need not be over. The bond which held the two of you together remains. Browning was right: "Grow old along with me, the best is yet to be." Being together is something not even death can destroy. Unless you let it.

Having been ejected from the ministers of England and imprisoned at Newgate, William Jenkyn petitioned King Charles II for release, his request being supported by physicians insisting his life was threatened by his confinement, was bluntly told by the king, "Jenkyn shall be a prisoner as long as he lives." A short time later it was reported to Charles, "May it please your Majesty, Jenkyns has got his liberty." Angered by the message, the king leaped to his feet. "Ay, who gave it to him?" To which the nobleman replied, "A greater than your Majesty – the King of kings."

Is it possible that the Greeks were on to some great truth when they looked upon death as a release from the prison of the body? There is sufficient evidence to convince the thinking person that getting out of prison is far better than staying in! Most of us find enough pleasure in our seventy years sojourn to overlook the fact of incarceration, but there are times when the bars do appear on the window and we wonder. Times when we cry, "Stop the world, I want to get off!"

When we sit by the bedside of one who is wasting away, conscious that she can never be released to go back to her family, it is easy to think of dying as being set free. In this vein of thought, there is no one who would prefer to live with the chains of pain and hopelessness when, if given a choice, she could flee this earthly incarceration.

DAY 53 . . . DAY BY DAY

Robespierre, the French revolutionary leader, who was guillotined in 1794 snapped in defiance, "No, Chaumette! No, Fouche! Death is not an eternal sleep! Citizens, erase from the tomb this inscription put there by sacrilegious hands, which casts a pall over the face of nature. Engrave rather this upon it: Death is the beginning of immortality."

It is to be expected that one's heart skips a beat at the thought of dying. Anytime we commence something new there is a degree of apprehension. To start a new job can be a scary thing. Getting married starts the butterflies in our stomachs. The birth of a first child fills us with awe. And the death of one known and loved across the years leaves us immersed in a silent mystery. These are all moments of beginning, excursions into uncharted territory.

To begin is to believe that what is taking place has the potential for expansion. At such a moment, no one entertains the thought of an ending. Nothing ended when you got that new job, wed that beautiful person or birthed that first baby. Each time your life blossomed into something more wonderful than you could have imagined. Could we but think of death as a beginning – not a termination but a regeneration – our perspective would be far more in line with reality. So, when you think of your loved one – and that is probably all the time – think of him or her as being more alive than he or she ever was. Envision him or her as being radiant with new life.

Just about everything has its breaking point. Beyond that, additional pressure is disastrous. A school pencil will bend only so far, in the hands of a lad, before it snaps into two splintered pencils. A limb, on a tree, will break when the wind is forceful enough. A willow will bend a lot further, but even a willow will finally give in to the strain.

No one would want to live in a world where no resistance is necessary. That is the stuff from which life is made. One lazy man was heard to say, "If it were not for stress, I wouldn't have any energy at all." But too much stress is too much.

People have breaking points just like pencils and trees. Some of us are already living splintered lives, lives broken from too much pressure. It is good when we can bend like the willow – and some of us are better at it than others – but no one can take more than he was made to absorb. Strain is not a friend to a healthy lifestyle. No one functions well when the strain threatens to break him. Be that as it may, we face the reality of living in a world where the pressures do become more than one can endure. Unless you and I are so emotionally wiry that nothing can damage us, we are in danger of being beaten to death everyday.

Learn to live with reality, but when the pressure gets too great . . . back off. There is nothing you have to prove. You can take only so much. And that is all that is expected of you. Learn to relax in the divine strength which is always available.

DAY 55 . . . DAY BY DAY

"*Whatever you do*, don't forget the batteries. They are on aisle seventeen." You have probably noticed that most of the toys wanted by modern kids are electronically operated. Dolls talk and walk by themselves. Fantasy world cars and trucks race across the floor, sirens screaming, bumping into furniture and bouncing back with a fury. I watch my grandchildren with their toys, and I always make sure I can defend myself against their living mechanical playthings. Sometimes I just hide!

I once got a toy tuck – must have been about six years old – with battery-powered headlights, which intrigues me for weeks. Now toys do just about everything . . . except breathe. That may be next. But invariably they come from the store with a note attached on the box: "Batteries not included."

It is interesting to observe that people are like toys in that, while we all have built-in batteries, they are quite often run down. A fun-down battery is as useless as no battery at all. But the wonderful fact is that there is a way to get re-charged.

Plug into prayer every morning. You will be surprised at how different your day will go. There will be a new surge of power which will be adequate for whatever you have to do. No matter how correct your life may seem, there will be nothing going on if your battery is down. My hope for you today is that your energy will be restored at the power source through prayer. The power is there, but you have to connect.

People who are grieving often ask, "Do you think I will know my departed loved ones on the other side?" Well, as Hamlet says to Horatio: "There are more things in heaven and earth than your philosophy has dreamt of." Nobody knows for sure, but as my grandfather used to say, "It is well within the bounds of reason to think that we will have as much sense there as here!"

During that interval between the death of your loved one and that of yourself, there is a lot of overlapping of the two worlds. We think about those on the other side and they think about us. No reason to assume otherwise. "It were a double grief," reasons Longfellow, "if the true-hearted, who loved us here, should, on the farther side, remember us no more."

One of my esteemed friends died recently, a big *little* man who stood barely over five feet tall. His ten year old grandson had asked him if he thought he would know him in heaven. When the answer was "Of course," the boy asked how. "I will have a glorified body," was the reply. "What does a glorified body look like?" came the follow up question. The answer was, "I'll be six feet tall!"

Whatever glorified bodies may look like, we may rest assured they will be fully recognizable. What would a family reunion be if nobody bore any resemblance to the way we remembered him? While there is often an identity crisis here, there is not the slightest chance of such a thing there.

DAY 57 ... DAY BY DAY

When I was quite young there was a song, which speaks more poignantly to me now than it did then. The climacteric words were: "Don't get around much anymore." Maybe you find yourself less ambulatory than when you were younger. Perhaps it is arthritis – the old demon that gets blamed for whatever we cannot diagnose – or just the passing of years. Hopefully, it is not depression. Possibly, you don't drive anymore or it may be that the years have confined you to a wheelchair. Whatever has shut you down, don't let it defeat you.

Unless some actual physical problem makes it impossible for you to "get around," you need to force yourself out of your room onto the sidewalk, into the fresh air, under the bright sun. Man is a social animal and you will suffocate without an open exchange with others. Find someone to share with and something exciting to do together.

When you can't go to the world, bring the world to you. Use your radio, television, newspaper, telephone. Don't let yourself wither up and die before your time if you honestly can't get around much anymore. A recluse is a miserable person. In addition to the outlets we have mentioned, let us not forget that God is our best friend. So, if you feel stuck at home, take advantage of the extra time to deepen your friendship with Him. That is so much better than sitting all day, in a stuffed chair, with nothing to do but worry about something we cannot change.

Over the triple doorways into the cathedral of Milan there are three inscriptions. Above one arch is carved a beautiful wreath of roses and under it is the legend: "All that which pleases is but for a moment." Above another is a sculptured cross with the words, "All that which troubles is but for a moment." But over the grand entrance at the center, above the aisle which leads to the altar, is the inscription, "That only is important which is eternal."

Millions of people have read those chiseled words, but few of them grasp their full significance until someone they love dies. Only then do any of us commence to reckon with that which is eternal.

What lasts when all we have treasured is taken from us? What is left when tragedy strikes and the radiologist shows us x-rays we would rather not see? Is there anything which remains when the world collapses around us? The interesting thing is that the things which are eternal are not things at all. William Ellery Channing saw this truth when he wrote, "Everything here, but the soul of man, is a passing shadow. The only enduring substance is within. When shall we awake to the sublime greatness, the perils, the accountableness, and the glorious destinies of the immortal soul!"

Even Charles Darwin once said that for those who fully admit the immortality of the human spirit, "the destruction of our world will not appear so dreadful." Only the eternal is important.

DAY 59 . . . DAY BY DAY

Duke Hamilton, a pious young nobleman, with a scientific bent, was discussing the subject of astronomy with his tutor. The prognosis on the duke's health was known to both men and it was not good. The conversation led to the nature of the fixed stars and, from the couch, where he was lying, Hamilton remarked, "In a very little while I shall know more of this than all of you put together."

When his death approached, he called his brother to his bedside and, addressing him with warm affection, said, "And now, Douglas, in a little while you will be a Duke, but I shall be a King!"

Standing beside an open coffin one is often heard to say, "Well, he is not suffering anymore." But, once in a while, we overhear someone say a much finer thing: "One thing is for sure, he is better off than we are." To be rid of pain is only a small part of what the dying person experiences. Absolutely *everything* is an improvement. Life will get better. Every religion known to the human race holds out the promise of advancement and growth beyond the grave.

French literary patron, Madame de Stael, entered in her wise sayings, "Divine wisdom, intending to detain us sometime on earth, has done well to cover with a veil the prospects of the life to come; for if our sight could clearly distinguish the opposite bank, who would remain on this tempestuous coast of time?" We have just enough insight and faith to believe that the yearning will not be denied to the children of God.

DAY BY DAY . . . DAY 60

Assuming that you began reading these thoughts about life and death shortly after the funeral, the time lapse has been about two months. How are you doing? Has it become any easier? For some, the answer is a qualified yes. The healing has begun. Others find it harder as the numbness wears off. At least, after this long you are in a position to take a seasoned look at where you are, and where you are going.

Wherever you are at this moment . . . is that the way you want to spend the rest of your life? If tomorrow is just like today, would you be pleased? Suppose the next two months find you right where you are now . . . how does that thought make you feel? The question is what are you going to do about it?

One of two things will happen – either today will be the beginning of a resolute return to life or it will not. Well-meaning friends are probably saying, "You have to get over it." That will never be the case. One does have to get beyond it. We have to walk through the valley of the shadow of death, but never can we permit ourselves to stay there. We must get through it, not over it. Beyond the shadows the sun is shining. On the other side of the valley are the upward slopes of the hills of God. It takes considerable effort, but the climb out of the darkness is not reserved for Olympic athletes. You can do it. You are made of that kind of stuff. The happy thought is there is a gold medal for everyone who does.

DAY 61 . . . DAY BY DAY

Receiving a gift is great fun. Whether for a birthday, an anniversary or just a wonderful surprise – we all enjoy opening gifts. Of all the gifts you have ever gotten, there is one which you receive all the time. And it is like us to thoughtlessly use it. I'm thinking about the gift of time.

At this very moment, we are in the middle of a segment of time which embraces 86,400 seconds. That is 1440 minutes or 24 hours. And it happens every day of the year. That is a lavish gift. None of us deserves such benevolence, such extravagant grace. What is even more unbelievable is that there are never any strings attached. You and I are free to use those precious minutes any way we like. We can use them to being joy and happiness to ourselves and others or we can use them to bring harm. The choice is ours.

Added to that, there is another way time can be used. It can be wasted. So much golden time is simply allowed to creep by. Needed rest and relaxation is not a waste, but careless indifference is! Look back for a moment . . . what did you do with those 86,400 seconds yesterday? Did you pine away in some dark corner nursing your wounds? Were most of them wasted on taking pity on yourself? To fritter away time on useless things is to lose it altogether.

There is a price tag on time. True, it is a free gift, but it becomes very costly when it is misused. It is the most valuable possession you have. Make every minute count today –all 1440 of them.

In the rock-hewn tombs along the banks of the Nile River have been discovered the words: "The dead shall live again." The Greeks acknowledged they knew little about what the other world is like – and so did the Romans – but they firmly believed in a future life. The Teutons of Germany and the Norsemen of Scandinavia believed in Valhalla, where the living dead would feast with the gods. American Indians were convinced there is a Great Spirit and a Happy Hunting Ground. Whether one looks in Africa, India or Arabia . . . it is difficult to find any group of people who do not believe in some kind of life after death.

"Whatever that be which thinks, which understands, which wills, which acts, it is something celestial and divine, and on that account must be eternal." Those are the words of ancient Cicero and they sound much like Jean Jacques Rousseau, eighteen hundred years later: "Had I no other proof of the immortality of the soul than the oppression of the just and the triumph of the wicked in this world, this alone would prevent my having the least doubt of it. So shocking a discord amidst a general harmony of things would make me naturally look for a cause; I should say to myself, we do not cease to exist with this life; everything resumes its order after death."

The constant refrain to the dirge of death is the triumphant song of life. Like a hallelujah chorus, from the soul of the human race, the song of life drowns the melancholy of the grave.

DAY 63 . . . DAY BY DAY

Automobiles come from the factory these days with a plethora of buttons and whistles on them, many of them so complex one has to read the manual several times to understand exactly what they do and how the operator can use them. Of course, all the old standard equipment is there – wheels, axles, frame, seat, bumpers and doors. And all cars, big or small, have gears. Whether manual or automatic, two or three shifts are employed in order to get the car going.

There are low, second and high, at least those three. Some of the automobiles have four speed transmissions and some have five; many have overdrive for easy cruising. Big trucks have *bulldog* for very slow, heavy loads. The fun part is driving in high or overdrive where the car floats along over the asphalt. Sometimes – and teenagers like this best of all – other gears have to be used.

There are days when you and I feel like we are in low gear all day long. No matter how hard we try, we can't seem to get going. Other days are smoother and more pleasant. If today is one of those bulldog days, take heart. Your load may be heavy for a while, but it will lighten as you move ahead. Hopefully, someday you can unload it entirely.

All of us face the grind at times. Slow days are just as good as the others. Maybe you won't go as fast or as far, but you are moving. Just so we don't sit still and burn up the clutch! That's the important thing. Don't quit.

Friendship! How wonderful is friendship. One true friend is worth more than his weight in gold. And he who has no friends, though he might be a millionaire, is the poorest person in the world. Yet, it is an unforgivable defect in man that he allows trifles to cool the fervor of one friend for another.

At no time do friends become so important as in periods of trouble. An old proverb puts it well: "A friend in need is a friend indeed." Think for a few minutes how so many wonderful people have stood with you during this tough time. There is no way you could have endured the blow, of seeing one dear to you die, without these "friends who stick closer than a brother" to undergird you.

The wise person treasures his friends every day, but it is when the floods of despair threaten us that those we take for granted are seen for what they really are. Ulysses S. Grant was in the middle of one of his difficult times when he remarked, "The friend of my adversity I shall always cherish most. I can better trust those who helped to relieve the gloom of my dark hours than those who are ready to enjoy with me the sunshine of my prosperity."

So many cards and letters, so many phone calls and morning visits, so many hours of weeping with you. Now it's your turn. Call that friend today and tell her how much she means to you. Tell her how she saved your life. Friends are the stuff out of which life is made and we dare not live without them.

DAY 65 . . . DAY BY DAY

Embracing her grieving friend, the woman in black kissed her wet cheeks and said, "I know it's hard, but life goes on." What she meant was, "Get a hold on yourself; you've got a lot of living to do." And that is correct. But such words mean more than just that. Anita Letitia Barbould's mind caught another wonderful truth.

> Life! We've been long together
> Through pleasant and through cloudy weather;
> 'Tis hard to part when friends are dear –
> Perhaps 'twill cost a sigh, a tear;
> Then steal away, give little warning,
> Choose thine own time;
> Say no, "Good night," but in some bright clime
> Bid me "Good morning."

Being able to continue with life in this world, following the departure of half one's life, is contingent on whether there is a certainty that the other half is alive, too. If I suspect death is the end, then getting on with life is nearly impossible. But, if I am confident that I will one day bid my loved one "good morning" . . . well, that makes all the difference in the world.

Life does go on. In more ways than one. Your loved one is getting on with life and – though it may be harder for you here than for that loved one there – you must not fail to live the rest of your life to the fullest. The only reason for the woman to wear black was because she did not understand what she was saying.

Healthy bodies may not produce healthy attitudes, but healthy attitudes certainly make a big difference in whether our bodies stay well. A woman, whose neighbor inquired about her health, dolefully said, "I feel very well, but I always feel bad when I feel well because I know I'm going to feel worse afterward." We have a tendency to make our good days less than they are by concentrating on the bad ones – some already gone, some not here yet. All we can claim, with any certainty, is this present moment. No other time is ours. Therefore, we must learn to live in the present and enjoy it. Leave the future alone.

If you feel well today, be thankful. Do not complain because you fear your good fortune will be sort-lived. Such fear is deadly. It paves the way for its own fulfillment. A merry heart is like a dose of medicine. It heals and brings about better things.

Learn to be cheerful. Yes, being cheerful takes some practice. For a few people, it comes naturally. For most of us, it takes a bit of doing when life becomes tedious. So, it is up to you. You have to refuse – deliberately refuse – to let anything that happens defeat you. Putting a torch to gloom is something you have to do.

Be good to yourself today. Stop pummeling your soul into despair. Live life to the fullest. Make it a point to let nothing blight this beautiful day. All days are good days. They only become bad when we interfere with the wonderful plans of a friendly world.

DAY 67 . . . DAY BY DAY

As we get older, what was once smooth, firm skin becomes loose and flabby. The muscle tone around the jaws and under the chin begins to disappear. Wrinkles appear around our eyes and in our foreheads and what we see in the mirror is not easy to accept. Most of us like the way we looked when we were twenty-five better than the way we look now. So, cosmetic surgery has become very popular. Growing numbers of men and women are going under the knife for what is often called a "face lift."

From what I hear from people who have taken measures to change their appearance, having a face lift not only makes people look better, but feel better as well. What is more needed than a face lift is a *faith lift*. One looks better when his spirit is buoyant. It is possible that you may be feeling pretty low right now. Life is filled with problems that have weighed you down and your spirit is flat on the floor. I hope this is not the case. But, if it is, take heart. God is the best specialist in the world. He can take the wrinkles out of your soul and the sag out of your spirit. What you need most today is a *faith lift*. It only takes a moment when you allow God to do His kind of surgery.

No anesthetic is required. It doesn't hurt. No such thing as being laid up in the hospital. And no big bill to cover the cost. The whole thing is free and it only takes a moment. There are many different ways to get in touch with God. Try one of them today and put youth back in your years.

Children grow up and move to a bigger city. Brothers and sisters become so busy with their own agendas that visits are further apart and even phone calls are neglected. Parents find themselves alone in a big house where the sounds of children are no more. Then the word comes that someone has died and, for the first time in years, cousins and old friends from the past show up. The reunion awakens the closeness once enjoyed and promises are made to get together more often or at least to write.

Since the funeral have you waited for others to contact you? One would expect them to do so. But it is so easy to fall back in the ruts we make for ourselves. Could it be that you yourself might write that letter or pick up the phone and call? Lonely people ought not wait for others to take the initiative. The tendency is to draw into our shell and lick our wounds, but there is no rule that forbids a lonely person from getting back in touch.

My mother used to tell me that God helps those who help themselves. Of course, He is always there for folks who cannot help themselves, but my guess is that you are not one of those. Reach out to family and friends. Take the offensive against the temptation to feel slighted or forgotten. The more you care about others, the more they will care about you. Loneliness is a one way street. If it is to be conquered, the traffic must run both ways. Happiness is a road that moves in both directions!

DAY 69 . . . DAY BY DAY

In one of the old inns in St. Moritz, Switzerland, there is an inscription which reads, "When you think everything is hopeless – a little ray of light comes from somewhere." Next time you think the night is darker than you have ever seen it, remember those simple words from the walls of that hotel.

Call that "little ray of light" whatever you like. Throughout these hints for living day by day, I have made frequent references to a divine Creator. Nearly one hundred percent of the world's people believe in some king of God. During times like these one becomes increasingly credulous about a Supreme Being. I call this "little ray of light", God.

He will never leave you in total darkness. Give Him the slimmest chance and He will illuminate your night. Never, never do you have to be a creature in the shadows. If God has his way, you will dwell always in the sunlight – the sunshine of his care. And when your life is covered by divine love, you never find it hopeless. There are bound to be times of discouragement, but there is no reason to make a steady diet of hopelessness. The saddest people in the world are they who refuse to come into the light. Insects may live under rocks, but not you. Soak up the warm rays of that "little ray of light" which comes, not from somewhere, but from Someone. If you have been living in a dark tunnel, look for that tiny beam of light at its end. It is shining just for you.

Now I want to suggest something very important. So listen up. Get yourself a cup of coffee and turn off the television while we talk. Think seriously about what I am going to say. Are you ready?

Go to town today and get a pet. That's right, a pet. A puppy, a kitten, a pot-bellied pig – anything you like. If you already have a pet, you are ahead of the game. Love it and care for it and thank it every morning for being your friend. But if you don't have one – get one. Not tomorrow. Today!

Even if you don't live alone – and especially if you do – you need a living thing which is your very own. No one is suggesting a dog or a cat can take the place of the person whom you have loved. That would never be the case. But having a living thing in the house, which you can touch and talk to – yes, talk to your animals – makes all the difference in the world for one who misses companionship.

Animals have a unique way of knowing when you are blue. A dog will sit with you for hours and listen to you talk about things you would never share with anyone else. A cat will lie in your lap and purr while you strike its soft hair and tell it how you miss that somebody. How much they understand nobody has any idea, but I think they know a lot more than you and I can imagine. They listen as well as a psychologist and they do not charge by the hour. No therapy known to man is any better. Go to town and get a pet. Now!

DAY 71 . . . DAY BY DAY

Accustomed as we are to viewing a departed relative or friend, laid out in a suit and tie or a beautiful dress, it seems to me that it would be more appropriate were the dress a cap and gown. When seen aright, death is graduation day. It is the beginning of something one has worked toward for years. Every ounce of energy has been invested in getting ready for this grand moment. The graduate is now about to enter the larger world he dreamed about during all those long days of preparation.

There is a reason why the occasion is called *commencement*. It is not the end! Students may shed a lot of tears as they face the thought of separation from classmates who have shared their lives for years, but none of them would want it any different.

Someday you will read in the paper that I am dead. Don't you believe a word of it. I will be more alive then than I have ever been. Death is commencement day, a festive moment of achievement and a time for congratulations.

Would it not be a pity to have to live here forever, on a planet seized by trouble and heartache every passing day? The world is a university of hard knocks and there should be no thought of resisting the day when those rough times will cease. When you think of your loved one – and that is probably every day – envision him in a cap and gown. Think of her receiving accolades for the completion of chapter one in the book of life.

DAY BY DAY . . . DAY 72

Idleness is the devil's workshop! If a person permits his adversity to knock him down – that's one thing. But if he never gets up . . . well, that's something else altogether. Of all the home-spun remedies ever given for despondency, the best is the admonition to keep your mind and hands busy.

Among the first signs of defeat is the sight of cobwebs in the workplace. This is particularly true of those who do not have to punch a time clock every morning. The path of least resistance is the one road we cannot afford to travel. Find something to do.

Find yourself a hobby or get a part-time job suitable for a person your age. Volunteer for community or church work. There are always envelopes to stuff, grass to cut, calls to make, errands to run. Find a needy family and bake them some bread or, better still, a calorie-filled cake. Tutor a child at school. Get you a pen pal and write regular letters or, if you have a computer, e-mail several every day. Hobby shops have hundreds of craft ideas and the materials for making them. Have fun making them and then giving them to your grandchildren or make friends of the neighborhood youngsters.

The scariest thing in the world is to see men and women crawl into their lair and hibernate for a long winter of sadness which never ends. Such people continue to exist, but they do not live. Even while they breathe they are withering away, leaving work on the bench which they should have done.

DAY 73 . . . DAY BY DAY

A *wise man once said,* "I think, therefore I am." Not only does that mean that if I think I have to be alive, but it also means "I think, therefore, I am what I am." We are pretty much what we think about. Bodily activity is spawned in the mind. Sometimes, hearing of some strange behavior in another, we say, "What was he thinking about?" And the suggestion that he wasn't thinking about anything is far from a correct answer. To do something thoughtlessly does not mean *without thought,* but without thinking the matter all the way through.

The body is the slave of the mind. What the body does is the result of a mental decision. That decision may be good or ill, but it is mind over matter every time. It is quite possible that, if you are feeling nauseous and weak – even experiencing pain in your body – your problem may be melancholia. There are medications on the market that are supposed to address this very real illness, but most of us can help ourselves by thinking right.

When I think better thoughts my health invariably improves as surely as it deteriorates from too much negativism. Happy thoughts make happy people; sad thoughts make sad people. The proverb is right: "As a man thinks in his heart, so is he."

How are you feeling as you read these words? The way you feel has a direct correlation to what you are thinking. What are you thinking? Whatever it is, expect your day to turn out that way.

DAY BY DAY . . . DAY 74

Enough time has elapsed now for us to talk about some practical things. Things like: Where are you going to live? Back home with your parents? Or will you move in with one of your children? Will you marry again, adopt a child, join a senior citizens club or start singing in the choir? It is not too soon to start planning the rest of your life. Otherwise, the weeks and months to come will buffet you between pillar and post and you will lose sight of any goal at all.

A rule of thumb is not to become totally dependent on someone else, but do not be too proud or headstrong to accept some help. Living alone, after having shared a home with someone else, is not the most pleasant lifestyle. You may not be able to tolerate living alone, but you might also find solitude better than noise and confusion. It must be remembered, however, that too much solitude is worse than noise!

As would be expected, most of the bereaved who read these words are older people, but death is no respecter of age. If you are now a young, single parent, you will have to decide who will care for the children while you work. Should you be a child now, without a father or a mother, you will have to grow up in a hurry and learn how to carry an extra share of the load.

Whatever the family situation may be, it is viciously disrupted when any member leaves. The trauma has been recurring for thousands of years and we always handle it. It takes much thought, effort and discipline, but you will make it.

DAY 75 . . . DAY BY DAY

Why do we laugh when we look at our high school senior class book? Because no matter how cool we looked then, our own teenagers tell us that we looked like nerds. How the years change everything. Fashions in clothing are forever in a state of flux. Hair styles? How silly those of twenty years ago look today, and how silly today's styles will look to our grown up grandchildren.

There is no known way to keep things as they are. One has only to look in the mirror to see that. But there are other ways, too. That empty chair at the table is a brutal reminder that nothing stays the same. The older we get the harder it is to change. The longer a happy relationship endures the harder it is to let it dissolve. Yet, we would not find a world where there is no change to be desirable.

We often think that it would be great, if we could keep everything the way it was when we were children, or when we were in high school, or when we first married. The world would be awfully monotonous if nothing ever changed.

Nonetheless, some of the landmarks do need to be spit-shined and kept around. How fortunate we are that God is the same in every generation. Our view of Him changes as we learn more about the way the universe is run, but as long as life lasts He will be at the helm of the ship of earth. He never alters his style. He is completely dependable. You can count on Him. So do it – with unshaken confidence.

DAY BY DAY . . . DAY 76

Among history's most illustrious men of letters was a renowned philosopher, scientist and publisher who lived during the days of the American revolution. Tolerant, urbane and intellectual, he embraced the Enlightenment without discarding his Puritan faith. At the age of eighty-four, in the year 1790, he died and was laid to rest beneath a headstone on which were chiseled the following words:

The body of
B. Franklin, printer,
(Like the cover of an old book
Its contents torn out
And stript of its Lettering and Gilding)
Lies here. Food for worms,
But the work shall not be lost:
For it will (as he believ'd) appear once more
In a new and more elegant Edition
Revised and corrected
By the Author.

Being of a scientific mind does not preclude a robust faith. The humble scientist knows that the scientist himself must surpass the boundaries of his limited knowledge. The mystery of life is bigger and grander than anything which can be compressed into these few short years. The universal intuition that man must have more time to fulfill his humanity is its own built-in proof of immortality. I just thought you ought to be reminded of this again.

DAY 77 . . . DAY BY DAY

Betty and I have both been married before. Jimmy was killed in a flaming highway accident at the age of thirty-one and Gloria died of cancer at thirty-nine. All of our parents are gone, too, plus other beloved family members and many cherished friends. So we know what you are going through.

For a while, it seemed like the natural thing to do was to keep everything exactly as our loved one left it. It was as if there were an oppressive sense of guilt if the least thing were changed. We have known people who preserve a loved one's room with nothing touched for years as a kind of inner sanctum, a holy place. Rooms, which are too sacred to change or ever use again, become sources of perennial sorrow and cast a somber mood over the entire household.

As soon as one can do so, closets should be cleaned out, clothes donated to charities, pictures put away. This is not done so you can forget. No one of us wants to forget . . . ever. It is rather so you can live again. For some, moving to a different house, where memories allow recovery, is the wise thing. Each person is different. It is simply a matter of giving yourself a chance to heal.

As long as we focus on sadness – especially items of sentiment that fill the soul with weeping – we obstruct the healing process. Exposing our minds to the things that produce happy thoughts is far better than cultivating sadness. When tending your garden concentrate on the roses, not on the thorns.

Outside the sky was dark, the wind was blustery and it was raining. Not the best kind of day for a funeral. My friend, a neighbor from just up the street, had died after a lengthy battle with an infection he could not conquer. Marvin was one of fourteen children, several of whom had come from a distance to weep with one another. At the foot of the coffin, amidst numerous flower displays, stood a large arrangement of red and white carnations. It was a wheel with fourteen red spokes. The rim of the wheel was missing around a half dozen of them denoting that Marvin was the sixth sibling to participate in the breaking of the family circle.

The broken circle . . . always a symbol of what death does to a family, leaves us speechless with emotion. The joy of keeping the family intact is short-lived. Sooner than we can believe, the circle cracks and a part of it is gone. The wheel never again runs as smoothly as it did, but it must never be discarded because a spoke is missing. The remaining spokes must fill in for the one which has retired.

Families, that have been close across the years, will inevitably move closer together and form a bond which heals the break. What are families for if not to do this? Every member is a part of something bigger than himself. Since that is so, the departed brother or sister lives on in the rest of us, never really gone at all. It is the family which insures the continuing identity of its parts.

DAY 79 . . . DAY BY DAY

Everything has its bright side and its dark side. The earth itself is dark on one side when it is filled with sunshine on the other. Your life and mine is a mixture of sunlit mountains and shadowy valleys. All of us must spend some time in the shadows if we are to appreciate the light. Shadows can be a welcome respite from the bright heat of the sun. Valleys are the most productive areas in the world. But no one needs to live in the valley all the time.

A good rule is to make oneself look on the bright side every day, even when going through the deepest valley of all. Every cloud has a silver lining. Too many of us see nothing but the gloom. No trouble is as bad as it might be. So lift your eyes from the earth and fix them on the heavens.

No one ever damaged his eyes by looking on the bright side. On the other hand, one can damage his entire spirit by dwelling on the dark. Every devastating storm in one's life finally comes to an end and the world returns to normal. The morning comes with regularity, but not until the night has passed.

Your heart may be filled with thoughts of loneliness, illness, poverty and a dozen oppressive things, but you can chase them away. Open your spirit to the sunlight and let the warm, healing balm come pouring in. Soon you will be singing, "Oh, what a beautiful morning, Oh, what a beautiful day. I have a beautiful feeling; everything's going my way." You can endure the shadows if you know the sun will rise.

During the weeks following a death in the family, there are times when one thinks he is coping with the heartache until some word or thought tosses him back in the doldrums.

If this is one of those down days when you are feeling like there isn't any use in going on, you are going to have to force yourself to think straight again. The accumulation of years, poor health, limited finances, loneliness, a feeling of inferiority – all of these and much more can zap your confidence in your ability to get on with your life.

My children used to love Watty Piper's book called *The Little Engine That Could.* It is a story about a talking train that faces tough, steep climbs with determined perseverance. "Puff, puff, chug, chug went the Little Blue Engine," writes Piper. Then, talking to itself, the little engine says, "I think I can . . . I think I can . . . I think I can . . . I think I can." And it does.

The old steam engine is a thing of the past, a nostalgia which our grandchildren do not share. Those of us who are older can hear those old engines straining every nerve to get going. "I don't think I can do this . . . I don't think I can do this . . ." Somehow those words don't fit the sounds of the might engines we remember. They don't fit you either. Keep on saying to yourself, "I think I can . . . I think I can . . ." For, when you really think you can you will. Defeat, with its companion discouragement, is largely a matter of the mind. Clean up your act. You can do it!

DAY 81 ... DAY BY DAY

"How sweet it is!" Those were the inimitable words of Jackie Gleason which inevitably brought down the house wherever he was performing. Do you ever feel like that? You can.

Surely, there is nothing which sparks the taste of sweetness any better than prayer. No, Gleason wasn't talking about something religious. And neither am I. Prayer is not a religious thing. It is rather an in-born need to communicate with something bigger than ourselves. One never needs to be religious to pray.

Days go much better when prayer is a vital part of one's agenda. Do not hesitate because you do not know *how* to pray. Who does? Just open your heart and lay out the petitions of your soul. Maybe there has been no thought of prayer during the last twenty-four hours, but it is never too late to try it. Nobody understands how prayer works, why it relieves our tensions, why it tastes so sweet. It just does.

We have talked about this before, but I know how prone all of us are to forget. Life without prayer is like not going to the doctor until you are at the point of death. When life slaps us down we forget about what's religious and what's not. We simply pray. It is the path of last resort. We are driven, brutally forced, to our knees. There is just nothing else we can do. How much better to engage in the sweet discipline before the doctor says, "You should have come much sooner." How tragic that we should wait until someone is dying to turn to prayer.

Epicurus argued that man dies like an animal with no hope beyond the grave. Therefore, he admonished to "eat, drink and be merry for tomorrow" they would die. Then there was Zeno, the founder of the Stoics, who was convinced that man has no future other than pain . . . hence, he must grit his teeth and clench his fists and bravely face his fate. Albert Camus was more nearly right when he said, "Man is the only creature who refuses to be what he is."

Man is more than an animal, grinning at adversity and eating itself into a dead-end grave. The human creature is a spirit – sometimes erroneously called *soul* – who has leased his animal body for seventy years – give or take a few. In our weaker moments, we give ourselves less credit than we deserve. Even at the open grave, too many of us are haunted by the question: "Is this all there is?" Such is to be expected as long as man refuses to be what he is.

The hope of life after death rests on the universal intuition that people are more than what we see, more than flesh and blood bodies that walk and talk. Something indefinable sets the human being apart from other creatures which roam the earth. To succumb to the idea that the life of a man or a woman ends at death is to sell ourselves short. There is more to us than that. Only unwarranted cynicism could induce you or me to be content with being less than what we are. This confidence you must have if you are to survive the ordeal you are facing.

DAY 83 . . . DAY BY DAY

"Look at that beautiful butterfly and learn from it to trust in God," writes Jeremy Taylor. "One might wonder where it could live in tempestuous night, in the whirlwind, or in the stormy day; but I have noticed it is safe and dry under the broad leaf while rivers have been flooded and the mountain oaks torn up from their roots."

Shelter from the storm. Could any boon be more welcome than that? The longer we live, the more frequent the storms. It is equally true that the older we get, the more dependent we are on havens we have not constructed ourselves. Although man has no way of knowing whether the butterfly worries when the skies grow gray with an approaching storm, more than likely they do not. Animals and insects seem to sense the coming of such things long before humans do. They know by instinct exactly where to go for safety. Under that broad leaf the butterfly confidently waits out the fury of the winds and rains above him.

For the person who grows up in an environment of love and trust, confronting the frequency of ill winds in later life is considerably easier because it is second nature. Confide in your friends. They are a shelter in the time of storm. And, above all, seek out the haven of the Eternal Spirit who has never left His creation without providing shelter for every emergency. God is the one fixed point in the universe. He never moves away from us. He is accessible, and He is easy to find.

We sometimes hear of somebody who claims to talk with the dead, but that is probably not true. At times, the two worlds do appear to overlap and we feel the presence of a departed loved one very close. But there is no evidence that the living and the dead actually talk to one another. That does not stop us from wondering, however, what our loved ones, on the other side, might say to us, if they could.

What do you think he would say to you? Or what would she say? Might they not say, "Don't worry about me. I'm fine." Following the death of my young wife, my concern was whether she were happy. It took a lot of talking, not to her, but to myself before I felt sure she was possibly happier than she had ever been.

The second thing would almost certainly be, "Why are you sitting there on your duff? Don't just sit there, do something." No better way is known for cultivating sadness than sitting and thinking about how it used to be. And no better way has been discovered for dealing with sorrow than that of staying busy. It doesn't matter too much what you do as long as it is legal and moral – helping others is about the most satisfying therapy in the whole world – but refusing to be a bored couch potato is an absolute necessity if you are to live again.

Finally, your loved one would probably ask: "Now that I have told you these two things, what are you going to do about them?" Good question.

DAY 85 . . . DAY BY DAY

So impressed was the poet Longfellow, by the work of Charles Sumner, jurist and senator during the Civil War, that he penned a verse especially in his honor.

> Were a star quenched on high,
> For ages would its light,
> Still traveling downward from the sky,
> Shine on our mortal sight.
>
> So when a great man dies,
> For years beyond our ken,
> The light he leaves behind him lies
> Upon the paths of men.

This is one of those undying poems which speaks for a multitude of men and women, not alone for the person intended. That special person may not have been famous while he lived, but he has left stardust everywhere we look. Nor can we think of her, who graced our days by her presence, without stars in our eyes.

People we love have a way of brightening up a room when they enter it. The atmosphere glistens suddenly with unearthly light. Nothing less than a miracle, that's what it is. Others envy you when they think of the one who was the light of your life. Be assured that the star who shone so brightly for you is shining yet. And be equally certain that multitudes of people still see it for it is impossible to bury the light.

A well-respected gentleman, whom I have known most of my life, was making some closing remarks as he retired from the company where he worked. He compared his retirement to the days when he played football in high school. As the team went onto the field for practice, they would pass under an archway over which hung a sign which read, "You have sixty minutes – no alibis, no regrets." Drawing the analogy, he said, "I have had my hour. And I have no alibis and no regrets."

What a fantastic way to live. Each one of us has a life to live and we must give it all we have. It does little good to offer alibis when it is done. Alibis never change anything. To regret a life is man's greatest tragedy.

Live each day in such a way that, if you had to live it over again, you would do it the same way! That's the kind of goalpost every person ought to set for himself. And, if we really live that way, there will be no regrets at the end.

Hone your skills. Sharpen your wits. Flex your muscles. Cultivate your spirit. Today will be a part of the past tomorrow and you certainly do not want to look back on today with the wish that you had lived it differently. The way to avoid such a tragedy is by resolving that today will be an unregrettable one. Make every minute count. That takes unrelenting will power and dogged determination, but the day deserves the best you can give it.

DAY 87 ... DAY BY DAY

She was only six years old when she died. The apple of her daddy's eye, little Molly was bright-eyed, cheerful and never met a stranger. In fact, she earned the affectionate nickname of "Little Sunshine." Hardly anybody called her Molly. It seemed like she wore a new outfit everyday, tiny dresses with pink ribbons and yellow frills. Little Sunshine's mother enjoyed nothing more than making the little pinafores and jumpers which showed off her pride and joy.

Then one day the sunshine began to fade. Molly was not herself, listless and uninterested in her lavish wardrobe, slow to get up in the morning and much quieter than usual. When Mommy finally took her to the doctor, it was discovered that Molly was very sick. The disease raced through her body and, within two months, Little Sunshine was gone.

The day after the funeral, Molly's mother gave all her dresses to children with whom she had played. The following day Mommy was back at her sewing machine. Her finger did not seem to move fast enough as the beautiful little garments came from her hands. Daddy would find one little girl each week, about six years old, from among the less fortunate families in town. And mother would make her look like a princess.

Friends soon asked why she worked so hard making the dresses. Molly's mother replied, "When I see the light in their eyes I know my Sunshine is still alive."

Both were very young when they married sitting in a buggy under a big shade tree near their hometown. Neither of their families had much so the two of them commenced their married life with little to support them except love. People say you can't live on love, but somehow they did . . . for over sixty-five years. As they grew old, one of them would often comment, "We've been married all our lives." And they almost had.

One day the angels came and the wife kissed her husband good-bye, anguish like she had never known tearing at her heart. She lived fifteen years after the death of the man she thought she could not live without. Of course, she had to. But never again was the woman her happy self. She brooded a lot and, once in a while, we would hear her say to her children, "Wish I could go on out there and get in that hole with your daddy."

What a waste! Counting the days – days which turned into months, then years – until she could die. Such people are dead while they live. And what they never understand is that such an attitude never helps anything. It has no bearing on the one who is gone. And it drives the remaining one deeper into despair.

Family and friends feel the gloom when around such a person. They avoid contact, which is the one thing the lonely need most. We are not apt to have many comforters unless we want to be comforted.

DAY 89 ... DAY BY DAY

The air was cloudy and damp outside the Peterson House, the streets packed with people, while inside had gathered the family and most of the cabinet. At exactly 7:22 in the morning the sixteenth president of the United States, was dead. Edwin Stanton, secretary of war, stood, hat in hand, by the bedside, tears gushing from his eyes. Without lifting his head, he was heard to say, "Now he belongs to the ages."

No one in that room was ready to give him up, but the inevitable had happened. The head wound was too severe to encourage any hope. And when the last heart beat flickered, Abraham Lincoln became immortal. He would be remembered around the world.

Your loved one is gone now, but he has left a legacy which all who knew him will remember forever. Our deeds live after us. A husband, a wife, a parent, a child – they all belong to the ages. And as long as one is remembered, that person is not really dead.

There may not be a memorial, in some conspicuous place, like that of Lincoln in Washington, but all those people who knew and loved the one you have lost for a while, will have built a place to kneel in their hearts. Whenever they see you, they will remember the one whom you think about all the time. Incredible as it may seem, that person whom you loved is not only alive in your memory, but in that of your friends as well. Your own heart should skip with pride as you realize what a prize you have given to the ages.

Our pilgrimage through the shadows of death now comes to an end. For some, the journey has been long; for others, we wonder where the time went. Together, we have ploughed deep furrows in the mind where thoughts of new life have been planted. Hopefully, we are more at peace with ourselves, more accepting of that which has befallen us.

Having one we love in another world makes the unknown less fearsome, in some ways more inviting. Our treasure is there. And our hearts are there.

What must now become the focus of our concentration is the joy of homecoming. William Cullen Bryant was thinking, in this vein, when he composed his classic poem, *Thanatopsis*.

So live, that when thy summons comes to join
The innumerable caravan that moves
To that mysterious realm, where each shall take
His chamber in the silent halls of death,
Thou go not, like the quarry slave at night,
Scourged to his dungeon, but, sustained and soothed
By an unfaltering trust, approach thy grave,
Like one who wraps the drapery of his couch
About him, and lies down to pleasant dreams.

This is the end of this little book. But it is still around. And that should be a lesson. Let us so live that when our bodies are gone, *we* will still be around. Death is transition. It is never the end.